# A very small book on American government:

A journey from reflection, to remedy, to hope

Written by Warren Burda
Illustrated by Jeff Sheldon

**Copyright © 2022**

# Copyright Disclaimer

***A very small book on American government***:  First Edition, Paperback
Publication Date June 2022
Publisher: Alpha Academic Press
ISBN: 978-1-948210-14-0

**Alpha Academic Press**

**Published in the United States of America**

# Introduction

I didn't plan on writing a book, and my friend, Jeff, didn't plan on illustrating one, but we did. My writing isn't perfect and neither are his cartoon drawings, but they work well together.

Teaching is what God called me to do. I did it faithfully for 44 years. My high school government students told me I should run for president and write a book. I chose their second idea.

The Founding Fathers gave us an amazing legacy of commitment to the blessings of liberty and to the Constitution. Since its ratification, we have had to decide how to respond to that legacy; testing our resolve to form and preserve a more perfect Union. Such decisions are not grounded on the wishes and whims of a few, but on the participation of many in the listening, discussing, and debating of ideas to find ways for government and the private sector to benefit the common good. When civil discourse works, it makes our nation better. Two-hundred and thirty-two years of trying again when it doesn't work makes us extraordinary.

Creating this book was both fun and thought provoking. It challenged us to think about our government, its role in our lives, suggestions to improve it, and our part in making sure it is secure for future generations.

Jeff and I hope it does the same for you.

*Warren Burda*

# Preface

"**I pledge allegiance** to the flag of the United States of America and to the Republic for which it stands, one Nation under God, indivisible, with **liberty and justice for all**."

In 1954 the words one nation under God were added to the pledge. President Dwight D. Eisenhower wrote that the addition "will remind Americans that despite our great physical strength we must remain humble…keep[ing] constantly in our minds and hearts the spiritual and moral principles which alone give dignity to man."

Dignity is defined as being worthy of respect.

That respect is evidenced each time "the government of the people, by the people, for the people" cares for the most vulnerable in the community and recognizes that when injustice targets one, it targets all. As Thomas Paine penned, "Give to every other human being every right that you claim for yourself."

*A very small book on American Government: A journey from reflection, to remedy, to hope* encourages all of us to be both competent and compassionate citizens. Sometimes We the People fail to do so (as did the Founding Fathers), but that should always be the goal.

The Preamble to the U.S. Constitution asserts that we strive "to form a more perfect Union." We may not be perfect, but we know we can get better – a little more perfect. And to that end, in the words of Eleanor Roosevelt, "It isn't enough to talk about peace. One must believe in it. And it isn't enough to believe in it … One must work at it."

Bound together in the common good, as informed and engaged citizens we have work to do, and we pledge to do this … with liberty and justice for all.

――――

*Dr. Dan Prinzing*
Wassmuth Center for Human Rights
Boise, Idaho

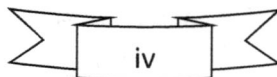

iv

# Table of Contents

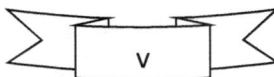

# Other books by Burda / Sheldon

*A very small book on K-12 public education:*
*A journey from reflection, to discovery, to revolution*

# Dedication

Jeff and I dedicate this book to our wives, Toni and Connie; to our children, Hilary, Kati, PJ, and Robbie; and to the United States Military, whose defense of the Constitution made the book's writing, illustrating, and publishing possible.

# A quote

*For having lived long, I have experienced many instances of being obliged by better information, or fuller consideration, to change opinions even on important subjects, which I once thought to be right, but found to be otherwise. It is therefore that the older I grow, the more apt I am to doubt my own judgement, and to pay more respect to the judgement of others.*

**Benjamin Franklin**

# Another quote

*To get nations back on their feet, we must first get down on our knees.*

**Billy Graham**

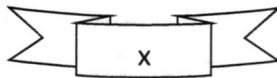

# PART I
## Reflection

# The K-12 years

Those of us who graduated from high school in 1971 remember celebrating the birthdays of Washington and Lincoln, Independence Day, Veterans' Day, and Memorial Day.

We remember that Washington was our first President but may not remember that Lincoln was our sixteenth.

We remember holiday parades, bands, drill teams, and the candy thrown from the floats; especially the candy.

We remember bomb shelters built in our communities. We hoped we would never have to use them.

Fallout Shelter

We remember watching the March on Washington and Martin Luther King. Jr. give his *I Have A Dream* speech - live on black and white TV.

We remember Blue Angel flybys at football games.

We remember using a home encyclopedia set to research reports about the signers of the Declaration of Independence.

We remember high school basketball games where almost everyone sang our national anthem.

We remember Presidential debates where the candidates didn't interrupt.

We remember trying to land on the moon first.

We remember memorizing the Preamble of the Constitution.

We remember voting for the first time but may not remember who we voted for.

We remember twirling sparklers and finding the perfect spot to watch the big fireworks show on the Fourth of July.

We remember the Cold War being anything but cold.

We remember the presentation of the flag, the playing of taps, and the shedding of tears as the remains of another brave soldier was brought home.

We learned that the Electoral College is a process, not a place.

We learned that it costs a lot of money to be elected President.

We learned that Washington didn't really chop down a cherry tree.

We learned that our parents used the *Magruder's American Government* textbook in their high school government class too.

And we learned that the Statue of Liberty is more than just a statue.

# Defining moments / realizations

It was my fifth grade year.
Waking home for lunch,
a girl told me JFK had been shot.
Mom and I watched on our TV,
in disbelief of what we were seeing and hearing.
Five years later,
we watched the same thing happen to Martin Luther King, Jr.
When they died,
America as we knew it died with them.

We used to put our leaders on pedestals. Now we put our opinions there.

Mom and Dad lie side by side in the Idaho Veterans' Cemetery. They loved their kids and grandkids, and they loved this country. I miss them both.

Mom served by helping at her neighborhood polling place and by giving tours to school kids at the State Capitol Building.

Dad fought in the Battle of the Bulge until artillery shrapnel took him down. Fifty years after the war,

Mom and Dad went back to Germany for a Battle of the Bulge reunion.The Germans marked all the allied crosses with a white ribbon.

They took Mom and Dad to the farmhouse where he was injured. It was still there.

Soldiers that once shot at each other drank together, shared stories of their kids, grandkids, and life experiences after the war; and remembered those who died in three and a half weeks of hell.

There were tears, forgiveness, laughter, and love. The reunion never made the local news back home, but Mom and Dad were OK with that.

Each time I look at Mom and Dad's head stones, I will give thanks to God for their lives, and I will think about the reunion in Germany.

In war, both sides showed the world how to fight, but at the reunion, they showed the world how to live.

The Founding Fathers had a clear focus of what they were trying to do - form and preserve a more perfect Union. It was the lens with which they scrutinized the value of every word in the Declaration of Independence, our first and second Constitution, the Bill of Rights, and the Federalist / Anti-Federalist papers. It was the lens that made their debates and compromises purposeful. When our Congress grapples with legislation, it would be well served by doing likewise.

I got to spend a day with Mary Beth Tinker. She was the guest speaker at a workshop on public policy. Mary Beth was thirteen years old when she and her brother wore a black armband to school to protest our involvement in the Vietnam War. Their simple act of civil disobedience would be the catalyst for a landmark Supreme Court decision on free speech in public schools. Their story got me thinking. If we want our children to be our hope for the future, we must regard them as our hope for the present.

The Framers of the Constitution discussed term limits for Congress, and chose not to have them, thinking that experience and the wisdom gained from it will benefit Congress. I would add another important reason. The Constitution should not be changed because voters are unhappy with Congressional election results. The people have spoken.

The People have SPOKEN!

Elections

DEMOCRACY!

I got the idea from how much fun my sons had with a big box of Legos. It was Thursday of the first week at evening school. My fifty-eight high school government students weren't all that excited to be there, but at least we now had a bigger room. I asked the students to gather in groups: those who like building things, those who like music, those who like art, those who like math, those who like writing, those who like drama, and those who like researching things.

I set my sons' big box of Legos down beside the students who like to build things; then directed the other groups' attention to tables where I had put writing paper, pens, butcher paper, colored pencils, markers, construction paper, crayons, scissors, tape, glue, a toy guitar, a tambourine, and a toy drum. The assignment was to answer this question: Why do we need government? I gave the groups one hour to be ready to present their answer.

The students engaged immediately, and the presentations were amazing. For the rest of the semester, there were virtually no behavior issues. The students did all their work in teams, using their respective gifts and talents to formulate and present a response to product prompts. All fifty-eight students checked the box for this sentence on the end of class evaluation: If my gifts and talents had been incorporated and celebrated in my classes K-12, school would have been so much more engaging and fun. Because of a box of Legos, my students were changed. And not only them. I used it successfully in my classes for the next twenty years.

Our Constitution was ordained to establish justice, but no matter how hard we try, we can't seem to get it right. We deceive ourselves and the truth is not in us when we elevate ourselves above others because of political party, special interests, race, gender, religion, or ability to use the gifts and talents we have been given. Even if we don't say it, we think they are less than us, and that our story matters more than theirs. We build walls around our positions and our self-righteousness. I and my become greater than we and ours. But God's welcomeness sees what is in our hearts and has no other side of the tracks. Imagine what would happen if the members of Congress, the President, and we who elect them, would simply love one another as He loves us.

We don't have a responsibility to vote, but if we don't, we could lose our sovereignty. And not only that. Each time a ballot is cast our nation experiences a new birth of freedom, and we honor those who have defended our right to do so - of which over a million have given us their last full measure of devotion.

Dad and Mom took the family to a (WW II) 99th Infantry Reunion, Checkerboard Division, held in Washington, DC.

Dad directed the reunion choir and Mom helped with the logistics. We got to sing at the World War II Memorial.

Many tourists there joined us in singing our last song- the Battle Hymn of the Republic.

When the song was over, we and they had tears in our eyes.

The infantry chorus would not have enough members to sing again. It was to be our closing ceremony.

No awards were handed out. No speeches were made, and the media wasn't there. But if the people at the memorial were listening that day, they would have heard more voices than just ours.

They would have heard the angels sing.

Every time a law is made,
no matter if it is good or bad,
we are less free.

# PART II
# Remedy

Part II honors the conclusion reached on page 30: If we want our children to be our hope for the future, we must regard them as our hope for the present. Its four remedies are made up of paraphrases of class work done by my high school American government students (pages 41-44), with my commentary interspersed.

# No. 1

# Congressional Riders

The Problem: Much has been said in civil discourse about Congressional Riders. The truth is that whenever one member of a body has the power to alter legislation that has gone through committee checks and balances and the checks and balances of debate and voting by the body in session, we have vigilantes loose in the halls of government. When that happens, government of the many becomes government of the few, and we are subject to laws in which our Congressional Representatives and Senators could not fully represent us. The Framers of our Constitution would have regarded this as dangerous and unacceptable.

Remedy:
1. Congress does the right thing and stops using riders.
2. The Supreme Court rules their use unconstitutional because we the people are subject to laws in which our Congressional Representatives and Senators could not fully represent us.
3. The Constitution is amended. (See Section 7 on page 42.)

# No. 2

# Healthcare

The Problem: Congress refuses to declare that healthcare is a basic human right. It substitutes the right to insurance for the right to health care. The Framers took great care to design the Constitution so that the powers granted to the Federal Government did not favor particular classes of people or special interest groups. Our current federal health care does the opposite. It is a for-profit system that favors those with higher income over those with lower income, thus denying, not supporting the availability and accessibility of comprehensive health care for all who live in this country.

Remedy:
1. Congress does the right thing and passes a joint resolution that declares healthcare is a basic human right in the United States, and that comprehensive health care shall be provided and accessible to all. The President does the right thing and signs the resolution into law.
2. Once this is accomplished, We the People hold Congress accountable to pass legislation that fully implements the resolution, and the President accountable to sign it into law.

# No. 3

# K-12 Civics Curriculum

The Problem: Our Founding Fathers understood the importance of an enlightened citizenry (wise electorate) and the role of civil discourse to that end. While there is compelling national interest in the quality of K-12 public schools, the responsibility for K-12 education rests with the states. Nationally, most states provide education on American government, but do not require the practice of that knowledge.

Remedy:
1. The teaching of high school American government must be part of the required curriculum of all states.
2. If we want our K-12 students to put into practice what they learn about our national government and the documents that pertain to it; then doing so must be part of the required curriculum in all states (as required labs in science classes are).

A personal note from the author: States do not have to reinvent how to do this. My high school government students enjoyed participating in highly effective programs (sponsored by the Center for Civic Education and The American Mock Trial Association) which can be done in the classroom or in state and national competitions.

# No. 4

# Loyalty to Party

The Problem: *However [political parties] may now and then answer popular ends, they are likely in the course of time and things, to become potent engines, by which cunning, ambitious, and unprincipled men [and women] will be enabled to subvert the power of the people and usurp for themselves the reins of government, destroying afterwards the very engines which have lifted them to unjust dominion.*
*George Washington- Farewell Address*


Remedy: The Constitution is amended with the following language inserted into Article I.

Section 1: ***Congressional candidates shall not have a political party affiliation listed for them on the ballot.*** (This shall be inserted above "Congress alone has the power to make laws." As per Article I, Section 4, the states will decide how to implement this into their Congressional election process. The writers of the amendment will need to set a deadline after ratification is achieved for all 50 states to comply.)

Section 7: ***Bills shall have only one subject. No Riders may be attached.***
*(This shall be inserted after "The Senate may propose amendments to tax bills.")*


A personal note from the author: There has been miles of talk about this problem in Congress, but little or no significant action taken. The Constitution is silent about political parties. I believe that the Framers intended for Congress's partisanship to be limited to being representatives of their respective states. Some may say that this remedy is radical, and they would be right. If the amendment is proposed and ratified, its twenty-six words will impact the forming and preserving of the Union for years to come.

# PART III
# HOPE

*The American dream belongs to all of us.*
Kamala Harris

# Setting the Stage

Achieving the American Dream is not easy. Nothing worthwhile ever is. Perhaps the greatest stumbling block to doing so is our tendency to think it is all about us and our greatness.

But the words of One born to a peasant girl and a carpenter proclaim a different kind of thinking: "If you want to be great, then you must be a servant of all. For whoever exalts themselves shall be humbled and whoever humbles themselves shall be exalted".

When visiting his restaurants, Dave Thomas (the founder of Wendy's) was known to put on an apron, find a mop and a bucket, and clean the restrooms. A mop bucket attitude, lived out by Dave Thomas and millions of others, built America, sustains it, and continues to fuel the American Dream.

Part III contains two true stories: The Students and The Pod. They represent the Dave Thomas's of their generation.

# The Students

# Introduction

The last five years of my teaching career I was privileged to teach American government at Sunnyside High School on the south side of Tucson, Arizona. The seniors in my classes were the most courteous, respectful students of my career. They didn't have much money, but they were rich in the things of life that matter - faith, family, and their Latino Hispanic heritage. Each day of class with them was filled with hope. Many were the first of their families to graduate from high school. Most registered to vote when they turned eighteen, and then exercised their right to do so. I am honored to include some of their work in this book. Each prompt involved extensive civil discourse, and the responses listed are the combined effort of fifty semester classes.

**The prompt: Determine one thing that will significantly improve the learning of American government.**

*We keep hearing that adults want us to engage in our political process so that we are a wise electorate, but those in charge of the high school curriculum don't seem to have gotten that message, or maybe they just ignore it. Practicing what is learned about our American government must be a required (not optional) part of high school civics curriculum.*

(This became No. 3 on page 36.)

**Prompt: Determine a remedy for Congressional use of Riders.**

*Congressional use of Riders causes the American people to be subject to laws in which our Senators and Representatives did not fully represent us. It's like someone is always trying to circumvent our Constitutional lawmaking system. We don't think the Framers would approve. The best remedy would be for Congress to voluntarily stop using Riders, but we have little faith that it will happen. The second best remedy would be for the courts to rule their use unconstitutional (reason given in sentence one.)*

*The third best remedy would be to amend the Constitution by adding these words to Article 1, Section 7: Riders may not be attached to bills.*

(This became No. 1 on page 34)

**Prompt: Determine a remedy for our national healthcare system.**

*According to the Preamble, we are to promote the general Welfare. Though there is debate as to what that means regarding healthcare, we believe it should be a basic human right in our country, and that comprehensive health care should be provided for all who live here. Our remedy has two steps. 1. Congress passes a joint resolution declaring health care to be a basic human right, and the President signs it. 2.Congress passes a law that implements the resolution, and the President signs it.*

(This became No. 2 on page 35.)

**Prompt: Determine a remedy for the problem of blind party loyalty in Congress.**

*Loyalty to a political party in itself is not a bad thing, but we believe blind loyalty to a political party is. It has severely limited the effectiveness of Congress as a lawmaking body by too often insulating them from what is best for the common good. Our remedy is amending the Constitution by adding these words. Article 1, Section1: Congress shall be a nonpartisan legislature. Its members shall not be elected with party affiliation listed on the ballot.*

(This became No. 4 on page 37.)

**Prompt: Determine the one thing that, if it were changed, would significantly improve public high school education.**

*We students, our teachers, and our school administrators have the least amount of say (legislated power) over the teaching and learning at our school. We see this as the cause of student disengagement and teacher and school administrator frustration/unhappiness. State education law and school district policy must enable students, their teachers, their school administrators, and their governing board members to work together in good faith to create (and later to make needed changes to) high school teaching / learning frameworks, which also should serve as the basis for teacher evaluations.*

# Conclusion

*Somewhere inside of all of us is the power to change the world.*
Roald Dahl

This quote describes the students perfectly.

They were not content to just learn about American government.

They wanted to practice what they learned, and they wanted the result of that practice to be included in the conversation of suggestions to improve our government, the study of it, and public high school education.

They did their part to make it happen, believing that our constitutional process of committee checks and balances and the checks and balances of debate and voting are worth participating in, and that our government, though imperfect, is worth our continued attempts to perfect it.

It was their gift to me.

Now, it is their gift to the nation.

# The Pod

## Introduction

Five neighborhood families in Olde Town, Arvada call themselves the Pod.

The age of the parents ranges from 34-41.
Their career fields are Career Advisor, 4th Grade Teacher, Physician Assistant, Master Electrician, VP of finance - oil and gas industry, Realtor (two!), Software Engineer, and Psychologist.

The age of the kids ranges from 3-8.

This is their story, in their own words. They have much to say.
I am honored to share it with you.

# Brooke (the writer) and Jimi

*Jimi and I are very fluid in our political party affiliations. When we turned 18 we consciously decided that I would register Democratic and Jimi would register Republican, so we could see both sides of the issues and understand what information was being propagated on party lines. Depending on the issue and how it directly impacts our family and daily lives, we often flow between the two parties. For example, we support Black Lives Matter (left leaning politically), but we are gun owners and support gun rights (typically a right leaning ideal). Additionally, I work for public schools and am greatly impacted by political decisions in education. I often lean left as the majority of my students and families come from underserved populations, but I also come from a family whose wealth stems from owning a private business; so the increase in taxes for higher income brackets directly affects my parents in a negative way.*

*We support BLM and deeply believe we have a responsibility to own our inherent racism and consciously work to be anti-racist, but find that we don't support all the actions of its members. We tend to look at events and actions of various political movements and determine what we agree and disagree with based on our own values and the impact on our lives and family. Other organizations we support (or have supported in the past) include but are not limited to: DCTA (Denver Classroom Teachers Association), United Way, Nature Conservancy, We Don't Waste, and Food for Thought.*

*Jimi and I did not participate in political campaigns this year. I have been active in school funding campaigns to pass a bond or mill levy taxes.*

*I'll leave talking about Congress, the Executive, and the Supreme Court to someone who might speak more eloquently than I can.*

Our Pod decision making process (when it happens) takes place at our weekly Friday happy hour after work. It is messy in the beginning with lots of questions, ideas, and some yelling, but we typically follow this basic protocol:

1. Identify a concern / need (maybe written on the pod school whiteboard or documented in our pod school google drive).
2. Pose the question or concern at the weekly Friday happy hour. Everyone weighs in (this is where it can get messy and loud).
3. Eventually we wind down and come to a consensus. Typically we propose a few solutions and then vote.
4. The final decision is documented in our pod google drive to refer to later.
5. If questions or clarification is needed we either ask them in our group communication platform (we use Slack) or revise at the next happy hour (update google doc).

* The most visited and discussed topic during school was around COVID protocols. It took several nights for the Pod to determine what we were willing to sacrifice for the good of the group, as well as how to navigate the ever-changing CDC guidelines (some of which we didn't agree with and so we created our own systems and practices that everyone followed).

*We don't gather with the intention of discussing politics, but current events often pop up while we're together. Here are some topics that have come up during our gatherings / happy hours (this is not an exhaustive list):*

- *Stimulus checks (various monetary distributions among the Pod) Child care and this year's tax credit (again, the various amounts distributed and how it relates to career / income)*
- *Public vs private schools (including charter, magnet, Montessori, expeditionary and distribution of funds for Title 1 vs non-Title 1 schools) We've also talked about the systemic racism in education and racial gaps in our area.*
- *A smaller section of the Pod, the 60th Ave neighborhood (because we are in sulots.) We read through each proposition and with our collective experience / knowledge we determined what the measures were actually proposing and weighed the pros and cons of each. We then made our decisions (not necessarily the same decisions in the end), but the discourse and various perspectives were incredibly helpful. For example, there was a Colorado proposition involving real estate. When I read it, I thought "sure sounds good", but when Kate and Kim explained what it would do to the market and how it impacted them directly, I changed my vote.*

*Jimi and I have a dream to live in a nation*

- *where all children (regardless of race, religion, or socio-economic background) have equal access to quality education and basic human necessities.*
- *where they can freely express their ideas, ask difficult questions, challenge the system, have new and innovative ideas, advocate for themselves, explore the world, be vulnerable enough to admit their faults, be compassionate and empathetic enough to see themselves in others, and let their experiences shape who they are and what the world will become.*

*I truly hope that my children continue the relationships we've built during this unprecedented year, and that they grow up to forge new, lasting relationships with a community of people like we have today. I hope they find friends that are like family, that love them unconditionally, that challenge them and push their thinking, and help them appreciate the gifts they have. And when they are together, may they be an unstoppable force for change!*

# Josh

*I am a fiscally conservative Democrat. I vote Democratic nationally and a mix of Republican and Democrat locally.*

*The organizations I support are non-violent. I believe we should all have a voice. We have the right and perhaps even the obligation to organize, and it is this right that keeps our country as honest as possible. Picking one voice over another leads to elitist right or wrong arguments. I think we can make sure that we listen to everyone and be as open minded and available as possible to discussion. That being said, I don't have any particular voice or group I support directly. I sponsor three children in South America as part of our family charity. I also support all firefighters and first responders, local food banks and VOC (Volunteers For Outdoor Colorado).*

*I believe Brooke covered Pod discussions thoroughly. Discussions around COVID and our protocols for traveling, visiting friends and family, how long to quarantine, when to quarantine, and mask protocols for traveling or ill families were definitely done on a consensus basis. Not everyone agreed with the results; but we all respected them because of our respect for each other. We all skipped some family meetings and get together with friends and made sure family members tested and quarantined before visits. I would say the Pod was completely successful since not one of us got COVID.*

*We didn't do a lot of political discussions. I believe everyone is basically liberal and we all generally align, some of us further than others. Personally, I don't discuss politics with many people as I find it creates unnecessary rifts.*

*I probably don't have enough to say here about Congress, the Executive, the Supreme Court, and issues I care about.*

- *I believe in human rights.*
- *I am not a fan of trickle down economics, but I do believe spending can get a little carried away on too many entitlements, especially locally.*

- *I am supportive of businesses and believe they should be able to operate with the economy and current social philosophies dictating their direction. I also believe in regulation, but have little faith in the ability of the government to carry out anything efficiently.*
- *My major gripes are campaign finance laws and no term limits for Congress and the Supreme Court. I tend to think fixing these two things would go a long way towards ending some of the corruption and misalignment that occurs in the government.*
- *I think Congress is self-serving and needs term limits in order to operate more in line with its original mandates, as representatives of us instead of representatives of themselves.*
- *The Executive should be a leader and a role model, someone you can look up to and want to pattern your life after - a hero in reality. This is pretty much never the case, so we are left having to deal with whomever is the most adept political maverick and choice of the power brokers. In this, the best we can hope for is someone who won't completely derail the country and will generally hit 60-70% of your personal ideological tenets. If there is room left over for outside wishes, then hopefully you can vote on character, but it is hard to find an election these days where character actually plays a meaningful role. Congress and the Executive have slowly but surely delegated their governing and lawmaking responsibilities to the Supreme Court. I am annoyed that it has become a political powerhouse. I think term limits for the Court justices will benefit the country, helping minimize the long-term effect of the Executive's power to recommend and the Senate's power to confirm.*
- *I am a gun rights supporter to a certain extent. I am not a fan of assault rifles and other weapons capable of mass murder in a short amount of time. I believe that arguments and rhetoric used to support such weapons being available to our gun loving culture, such as protecting ourselves from martial law and government takeovers, are not relevant.*

- *I think marijuana should be legal and treated the same as alcohol. Marijuana's drug prosecutions are wreaking havoc on thousands of families.*

*I have not participated in political campaigns nor am I registered with one party. I'm a free agent.*

*I hope that my children have equal opportunity and fair competition for jobs and life itself. I hope they grow to be responsible, contributing, and considerate members of society who fight for what they believe in and stand up for others who cannot. I hope they do not judge, but do what is right. I hope America provides my children the opportunity to work hard and reap the benefits of their work. I hope they do a little bit of blue-collar work and retain humility for those who do. I hope they have to earn what is theirs. I hope they learn that voting is a right and a privilege, and that if we don't exercise that right, we could lose it. I have lived in France, Italy, and England and visited many other countries. I consider America to be the greatest of them all, regardless of our faults. As fractured as this country is, I would still rather not live anywhere else.*

# Kim (the writer) and Brian

*I am a registered Democrat who typically votes Democratic at the national level, but mixes it up locally and during the primaries. I would love to have more opportunities to vote outside of the two parties, and I was hoping Trump would split the Republican Party in two so that maybe we'd have at least three people up on the debate stage. I am appalled at the amount of money that goes into campaigns and lobbying. Often campaigns are built on fear, fear of people taking your rights away, hurting your family, or taking what you are owed. We have built this notion that there is a limited supply of money and power and to give to all we must give up ours. I think the mindset needs to shift to abundance to give us any hope as a prosperous country. I wish to see taxes going towards more public services like transportation, physical and mental healthcare, higher education and affordable housing. I don't have a fix for most of the injustice I see, but feel that the US is doing it wrong. I believe we as a nation have failed to provide equal opportunity to the majority. We have spent decades ensuring the wealth gap continues to increase. I see the rates of hungry adolescents, homeless, unemployed, people on welfare as failures from our central government. There is real reform that needs to happen nationally, but I fear the US is too divided, selfish and uneducated to make the real changes we need. As for gun rights, I don't understand why you need a semi-automatic weapon as it A. escalates the situation and B. is made to kill. But if you truly feel the need, intense background checks, licensing, and accountability need to be there.*

*I'm honestly in search of organizations to support. I feel like the past year has been pretty transformative and eye-opening for me. I am ashamed to say I really never thought much about anything political outside of Planned Parenthood. And that was just because it was related to women's rights and always on the debate platform. After the George Floyd murder, I became more aware of the racial injustice in this country and supported BLM. We need better support for our police, better training, better mental health support for the entirety of this country. I went to a fair housing webinar and then read "The Color of Law" which opened my eyes to the de jure racism and segregation generations of families have had to endure. I'm starting to research how I can get involved in keeping housing affordable, ensuring teenagers are financially literate and able to invest in their futures regardless of SES. We also donate to CPR each month, as I believe they are the least biased news outlet I can find. I'm not here to debate or change anyone's mind... I just want the world to be a little kinder.*

*Brooke did a good job covering how the Pod made decisions. BUT personally, it was a very different experience with the pod being in our house. There was a lot more management of guidelines, expectations, and overall administration that Brian & I didn't really realize we were signing up for. We set up the school in what would have been our office as we had just moved into the house, so we didn't have clear rooms defined yet. Our dining room, drink fridge, and pantry were taken over by school food and lunch items. I separated sections of the basement, so our kids didn't have to share ALL of their toys. There were specific school toys and Beaumund boys' toys.*

*Lacie & Jake needed before/after school care 3 days a week, so we volunteered to make breakfast for their girls and had them hang out after school until Jake could pick them up.*

*We didn't anticipate that we had to regulate when the pod was in session and quickly had to set expectations that if real school wasn't in session, our pod was not available. This was less of a democratic decision and more of a mandate over a zoom call. Our house was not a daycare, and kids and facilitators should get breaks during the designated breaks (including a couple debated snow days). Certain expectations of cleaning up snacks and school supplies so the next day facilitators were ready, and our house was back to "home" was another mandate. Brian would order Costco every Sunday and empty the dishwasher every morning, so the house was ready for Pod time. I also felt an unwarranted obligation to ensure substitute facilitators were managed and often took the open shift as my schedule as a realtor allows me the flexibility. Realizing that I was no longer giving myself any time to do my paid job during pod hours, I eventually stopped picking up all open shifts and let the parents who needed coverage figure it out.*

*I think it'd be interesting to see WHY everyone did the pod. Our reasoning was control and risk-management. Brian & I had worked out an incredible working schedule where we would need very little childcare. When we started getting communications about what school would look like with COVID protocols shutting down whole classrooms 10 + days at a time, the unknown of how harmful COVID was/wasn't to the kids, the cancellation of all specials, lunch, recess AND the delay in starting in person to begin the year we decided Kate's idea to start a pod was much better! It was a no brainer for us, we were going to be home with our youngest anyway and this way we reduce our exposure to just certain families. But the sacrifice was we didn't travel to see friends and family, missed new babies, holidays, and distanced ourselves from some of our closest friends.*

*What makes our group work is the respect we have for each other as individuals. So when political differences arise, or when Jake doesn't want to come to the debate watch we get it :-) It was interesting to do this during such a heated election year as a lot of discussions came up during the voting process and debates we watched. I really enjoyed going through our local propositions and discussing what it would mean from different industries and political views.*

*For me, any political discussion with friends was not to change their mind, but to understand their perspective. It is very easy to demonize all those that voted for Trump, but when one of your dear friends, raising amazing children in your pod, voted for Trump you realize it's much more complicated. It was also interesting to talk about our parents' politics as well.*

*I agree with a lot that Josh had said, the executive branch has been / is a huge disappointment. It's all talk for votes, and nothing else gets done. The first term of a president is just a 4-year political campaign to get reelected. It's exhausting and disheartening. I honestly never took an American government class in high school (loophole in changing states, I took it in middle school which was WAY too young). I wish I had a better understanding of what makes our system so broken, but from my perspective it's term-limits, lobbyists, and campaign money. The lengthy bills to ensure everyone is happy and everyone gets to benefit (often not even relevant to the bill) helps the greediest win. The career politicians know how to work the system, but the system is built for the top to stay there and the bottom to work their ass off for a crumb.*

*The two-party system makes everything more polarized. If COVID in an election year taught us anything, we as a society are doomed. I don't say this to be hyperbolic, but the fact that scientists gave us the tools to help protect 100s of thousands of people from a deadly, unknown virus and over half the nation refused to wear a mask or get vaccinated based on what political party they aligned with, is just hopeless.*

*I have not and am not involved in political campaigns. I could probably get behind something local, but nationally the parties are too big, too polarized, too two-partied, too focused on making their benefactors happy to really make THAT big of a difference in my daily life.*

*Voting rights & minimum sentences go hand-in-hand. They need to be reformed. Our prisons are full of citizens who should have the right to reform, educate, earn a living and VOTE. If parenting has taught me nothing else: punishment doesn't work.*

Taking away rights forever does not motivate the individual to be a better human, it is demoralizing. Give felons a chance to reenter society with education, mental health support and jobs.

Marijuana- decriminalize it, tax the, you know what out of it, empty out the prisons and use those taxes to pay our teachers better so our little humans are better educated and actually have more equal opportunities.

Climate change- it's real, it's probably too late, but we should at least try. Big money should invest in renewable energy. Finite industries need to change with the times. We have been so quick to move to 2-day shipping and put the local stores out of business, but we can't fathom shutting down a coal mine. Humans CAN evolve. We can learn new trades and technologies.

I think it's important to know that although we were all friends prior to the pod, we were not THAT good of friends. We would hang out occasionally doing game nights or we'd watch a show together. But this pod brought us together in a way I never expected.

I, personally, learned to voice my opinion, wants, needs and learned to say "no". We all have different backgrounds and ideas around how to parent, but our intention was to give our kids the best year we could give them. We all have our own styles and political views, but we are all trying to raise good humans. We hold all of our kids to a higher standard than ourselves, we all want the next generation to do better.

*I posted this on FB at the end of the school year:*

So when we say we had a pod this year...

Last year it was unclear whether or not school was going to be in-person, partially in-person or fully remote. We then bought a house closer to friends and decided we should do remote learning at our new home. The intent was simple: give the kids stability in an unstable world. Give us the stability to know when we can work and when we need to help with school. Five families came together and we set up desks, posters, centers, white boards, and a library.

We all took pod shifts, set protocols, student jobs and guidelines, created lunch, art, international days and read-a-loud schedules. Our kids shared their parents, their home, their space, their toys. And for what? 8 new brothers and sisters. As parents we also made sacrifices, but this tribe we created out of necessity has become a beautiful "chosen family". I never wanted more than 2 children, but now we have 10! I do not hesitate to discipline or comfort any one of these children. They drive me just as crazy as my own kids, I know their pain vs whine cries, and they ask the nearest adult to mend their wounds.

The strength and courage it has taken for all of us to keep this pod healthy has caused family feuds, friendship strains, late night debates and marriage challenges. But we did it! We not only survived, but thrived through 175 days of remote learning. Our kids had a pod to play and learn with. The relationships I have formed will be lifelong. This was our school, childcare, support system, pod, and family. We trusted each other to uphold our CDC inspired protocols to keep us and our children safe. We had quarantines, mask days, and frequent testing. We worked together to respect everyone's comfort levels. Sometimes we were even stricter than CDC guidelines. We got quorum approval for travel and visitors. We missed so many non-pod birthdays, holidays, weddings, and baby arrivals. But we stayed COVID-free and that was top priority for us.

The first few months were difficult to say the least. Feeding 10 children took a half hour to set up (now it takes 10 min). Amazon 2-day shipping was a lifesaver for the "ah-ha" headphone splitters and extenders, black markers, dongles and HDMI cords. We had organized PE lessons until we realized recess should be a break for teachers and kids. We had preschoolers napping too long. We started with parent read-alouds, now the kids take turns reading to their peers. We lost numerous preschooler help and remote teachers. We rearranged desks and schedules. Classroom management is an art: Dojo points and "1-2-3 eyes on me" are lifesavers. In the end we were a well-oiled machine with morning messages and weather, simple snacks, center time, group projects, movie days, Go Noodle indoor recess, international days, field trips and art with Memaw.

We used slack for parent announcements, sharing funny or stressful stories & artwork. We had a Google Drive with protocols and 700+ photos. We all learned how to navigate Seesaw, Zoom, Epic!, Dreambox, Splash Learn, RAZ Kids, Tynker, Peardeck, Chrome Music Lab, Flipgrid and Amplify.


We quickly learned:

-snacks should not have dip

-Costco orders have a lot of boxes (any extra recycling room?)

-lost and found is necessary because of the amount of SOCKS discovered throughout the house

-happy hour is the perfect forum to make school decisions

-refer to the Google doc as it has the group decisions written down when happy hour turns to hrs.

I will be forever grateful for this pod. This chosen family of ours has made this last year successful both personally and professionally. It is bittersweet to get our home back. Now what to do with this empty classroom!? 🩶

*There have been times when we talk about just leaving. That this country is so broken and it's too big to actually make a difference. Our country is so young and innovative, but we're crippled by greed and companies and banks that "are too big to fail". But our country is having the hard conversations that a lot are not and some just cannot. I appreciate the fight for equality across race, gender, sexuality, and disability. I have to keep reminding myself that our nation is a teenager at best. But if we don't choose to change, we're going to fail and it will be devastating. I want to see our country succeed and LEAD by example. I want to be proud about the country we live in and the decisions we make. Our history classes present the great nation we have become, but we are not great. We have the potential to be great, we have the tools, we have the technology, we have the ingenuity, we have the passion and we have the money. Just look at the incredible technology and medicine that has come out of this great nation. May we continue to strive for equality, justice and opportunity for all. We don't need to bring people down to bring others up, we can all grow together.*

*For my kids, I hope they grow up in a kinder, more understanding world than we did. I hope the bullies they encounter get the mental health support they need. I hope they don't have a I vs. them mentality but a us vs. past us. I am raising two white, blue eyed, blonde haired upper middle-class men. I hope we can raise them to be compassionate and empathetic. I want them to follow their hearts and do what's right. I want them to live in a world where they can wear a Jo-Jo Siwa pj set (found in the "girl" section) because they really love her music. I want them to continue to dance with the freedom of no judgment. I want them to feel uncomfortable and grow from their mistakes. I want them to see the world's diversity as interesting and beautiful. I want them to always ask questions and be curious. I want them to find their people, who will challenge them, hold them accountable but love them unconditionally.*

*The world is rough out there, people are doing the best they can with what they have. And people are in constant need of the benefit of the doubt. My job as their mom is to provide a safe place for them to come home to. They can cry when they are hurt, yell when they are mad and snuggle when they are upset or in love.*

# Lacie (the writer) and Jake

*I am a registered Independent, but lean Democratic on most things. Jake is a registered Republican, mostly for gun rights purposes, but also swings more liberal on many issues.*

*We believe in being kind humans. We both support Thin Blue Line and well as Black Lives Matter, even though they don't often coincide. We are vegetarians by choice; mostly for environmental reasons, and some animal rights reasons as well.*

*To add on to Kim's comment about WHY everyone joined the pod: We had similar reasons to Kim and Brian; I think we all did. Jake and I do not have jobs with flexible hours and are definitely not able to take 10-14 days off without notice to be home with our children to facilitate remote learning each time their class would have to quarantine. We also wanted to have some control over COVID exposures to protect our family, and again, be able to continue working (because if anyone in our family became sick with anything, COVID or not, we would have to be out of work for 2 weeks). Jake and I each worked 4 days per week already, so it made more sense for each of us to volunteer our day "off" to the Pod School, so we could continue working our normal schedules otherwise. So, every Tuesday, I was at the Pod all day, and every Friday Jake was. It worked out, because we didn't have to miss any work for quarantine and NO ONE in our family got sick, with anything!*

*The Pod was both amazing and very difficult, a life saver and a relationship challenger. We were able to stay healthy the whole year and continue working without any quarantine, which is incredible. Spending an entire day with 10 children, each with different schedules, feeding 10 children 3 times per shift, learning how to best interact with each child, was draining and rewarding at the same time. We became so close with these humans, we became a family. It's really amazing how well we actually got along and made our plan work, thrive really.*

*On the other hand, we had other relationships that really struggled from this. We had some loved ones who felt differently about the pandemic/COVID, and just couldn't see why we were doing this and why we couldn't see them (due to the guidelines we set up to reduce COVID exposures). That made this feel almost impossible at times, but we made it through. We are still very close with the Pod months after the school year ended, and I expect we will be forever. It really creates a bond when you go through something like this together. We are mending the relationships that struggled while we were in the thick of it, though there remain differences of opinion which will probably never align on this topic, unfortunately.*

*I think my dreams are unrealistic, unfortunately. I would love for them to have a world where people would stop politicizing everything; including science and medicine and see the facts. I hope it's not too late to turn some things around with climate change and the state of our planet. I hope we find good alternatives to things like plastic, Styrofoam, fuel / energy, etc. that can be made mainstream, and people actually accept and use them. I would love everyone to just get along while understanding and appreciating our differences rather than hurting each other, both emotionally and physically, over them.*

*I hope my children will be kind, compassionate, and empathetic humans. I hope they find happiness and love in whatever direction they go with their lives.*

# Kate (the writer) and Robbie

*I am probably about as liberal you can get on most matters, though I am a registered Independent. I am a firm believer in women's rights and social & economic equality for women. I am also passionate about immigrant rights and giving more legal pathways for refugees and immigrants to become citizens. I believe that those of us who have more have a responsibility to do more for others with what we have. I am a strong advocate for police reform and reallocating funds that are distributed to police for more social services and mental health support. I do not personally like guns, but I support responsible gun owners' rights to have guns and have written to our congressmen here in CO in support of a 24 hour wait time for those applying for guns as well as full background checks as part of the application process. I also believe that no citizen should have the ability to buy an automatic weapon. Lastly, I am passionate about tax reform and a more equal distribution of wealth, particularly at the local level.*

*I am a strong proponent of Black Lives Matter and the Innocence Project. One of my biggest beliefs is that "White Silence Equals White Complicity" and that those of us with privilege have a responsibility to speak up for those who have no voice in the system. I was very inspired after reading Just Mercy by civil rights attorney Bryan Stevenson and White Fragility by Robin DiAngelo. Just Mercy is about Bryan Stevenson's involvement with trying to exonerate innocent (mostly black) men who are wrongfully accused of various crimes and have been sentenced to death. Write Fragility posits that inherent racism is real and it is only when white people acknowledge this and work towards an anti-racist framework can real change occur.*

*Currently, I've been very active in the campaign "Justice for Elijah" which is seeking to bring to justice the three Aurora Police Officers and two paramedics who inadvertently killed Elijah McClain with a combined use of force and Ketamine (which has since been banned as a means of use for the APD!) as he was walking down the street on August 24, 2019. He succumbed to his injuries on August 31, 2019, two years to the day from which I write this. He was only 23 when he died. Robbie and I also support, on a monthly basis, Colorado Public Radio because we believe in quality, unbiased news sources and the American Foundation for Suicide Prevention, as they work towards providing FREE mental health services for those in need and at risk of mental health crises.*

*Politics do come up. I definitely don't agree with several members of our pod on guns, but it has proved to be a safe space for us to talk about our differences in a respectful way. There have been several evenings that we've talked about individual gun ownership and even though we don't agree, we can say to each other, "That's interesting, tell me more about why you think that," and being able to actually listen to my friends on this issue has made me understand and support why they personally own guns.*

*I agree with most of what Josh said, especially about Congress. It seems like the longer one's in Congress, the more out-of-touch he/she becomes with what "regular" people need and want. I believe most of this is because as one's socio-economic status rises, they forget that not everyone has the privileges that they now enjoy and forget daily struggles that many people have. If they themselves are not experiencing the same daily struggles, it becomes more difficult for them to have perspective on what would make an actual impact for good. I also think that there should be term limits and the filibuster shouldn't be allowed to be used anymore because it is abused to the point where very little action and policy can actually be made in Congress.*

*I personally believe that our two-party system has become a broken system and everything is so politicized now that you feel like you have to "pick a side."*

*I believe that social media has a lot to do with that and it's our inability as humans to have a respectful dialogue with those that don't agree with us. That is one of the things I am most grateful for with this pod is that we can respectfully disagree and actually discuss.*

*Regarding our President as executive chief, I believe its role is primarily symbolic and the real change comes at the local level, district-by-district, state-by-state.*

*On marijuana, I hope that not only is it legalized but that all incarcerated people who are there for non-violent and low-level drug offenses are released and their records expunged.*

*On voting rights, I wish that the rules were the same on a Federal level because voter suppression, depending on what state you vote in, can be a very big issue and deeply affects communities that are traditionally disenfranchised. Being able to vote should be easy and regulated on a federal level. Again, this is why I believe that local government is so important and who we vote for on a local level is so critical. Representation matters.*

*I was very active in Barack Obama's political campaign in 2008. I was 22 then and his campaign symbolized progress for me, especially as a Chicagoan at the time. I campaigned for him in a traditionally very "red" suburb of Indiana called Fishers, and went door-to-door trying to convince voters to vote for him. In 2008, he won that district and this is one of the times in my life when I realized that my actions can make change. This was a huge lesson for me. Robbie and I, along with a few of our friends, were among over 200,000 people in Grant Park the night he won, and what his win symbolized for Chicagoans, particularly black Chicagoans, is something that can't really be put into words. The feeling that night was visceral....you knew it represented something deeply profound. This year, I did a few days of phone-banking for the Biden/Harris campaign because, while they were not nearly my first choice, the election of Harris as VP also symbolizes progress for me.*

*There are many decisions that she made as DA of San Francisco and AG of California that I do not agree with, but like Obama's election in 2008, her election in 2020 embodies progress. Representation of people who are traditionally underserved or unrepresented, like women and people of color, really matters. THAT is progress and I always want to be a part of that progress.*

*Phew, what a question! How much time do you have? My dreams for America:*

- *We prioritize and incentivize individuals and corporations to use as few fossil fuels as possible, and that renewable energy sources become the norm (i.e tax incentives for EVs, Solar and Wind Energy, powering homes with electric heat pumps and geo-thermal heating/cooling, incentives for eating less or no red meat). There is no denying that climate change is real and I worry that there will be no planet worth living for as my kids grow old. I especially worry because those that will be most affected (and are already being affected and displaced by climate change) are those that are the most economically and socially disadvantaged.*
- *We work towards equality for all by acknowledging that while we are a great country and we enjoy many privileges, we are undeniably a country whose economy was built on the backs of slaves and on stolen land. While our motto is "equality for all," that is not our de facto reality and it takes our collective activism to do everything we can in our policies to make it better, particularly at the local level. Paying attention and knowing our city council members and what they stand for as well as our local district attorneys and Attorney Generals is imperative.*

**For our children:**

*That they always advocate for themselves and for those that can't advocate for themselves, and that they, as John Lewis says," Make good trouble," in all things. I also hope that they find and know joy in their lives and that they feel the freedom to be able to fully pursue whatever they want in life. I also hope that they find their community of individuals who support and love them unconditionally.*

# Conclusion

The Pod's use of civil discourse rivals that of the Founding Fathers.

The Pod's content of character drives their civil discourse,

not the other way around.

They are honest.

They have each other's backs.

They celebrate what's right with the world,

but do not ignore what's wrong with it.

They are grateful for what they have.

They help others who are not as fortunate.

They seek to be a wise electorate.

They are hopeful; refusing to let the divisiveness, hatred, and negativity of

this world have the final say -

for their families, for each other, and for this nation.

It doesn't get much better than that.

# The Table

Benjamin Franklins' words "if you can keep it" loom large before us as one thing after another tests this nation's ability to long endure, Covid 19 being the latest.

If You Can Keep It!

Giving our best effort to battle the pandemic or any such adversity depends on our collective willingness to come down from the bleachers of exclusiveness and indifference to the table of inclusiveness and goodwill.

It is there that the tendency to use hateful political rhetoric can yield to words of kindness and compassion.

It is there that the tendency of public officials to use power in self-serving ways can yield to servant leadership.

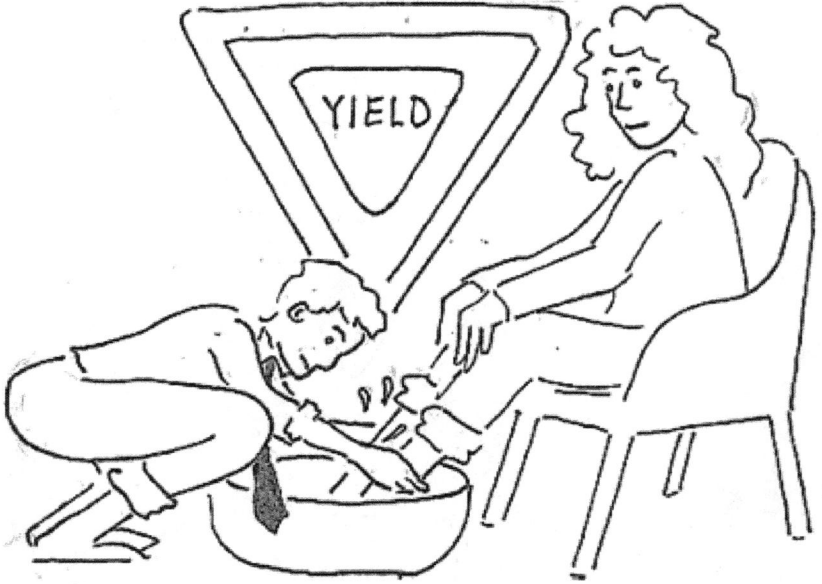

It is there that the tendency not to discuss political / public policy disagreements because of others' refusal to listen with an open mind can yield to respectful civil discourse, discernment, and compromise.

It is there that the tendency to take our freedoms for granted can yield to thankful appreciation and support for those who put their lives on the line to defend our right to have them.

It is there that the tendency to be inattentive to the disenfranchised among us can yield to advocacy on their behalf.

And it is there that the tendency of voters to over-rely on loyalty to factions (political parties, special interest groups, and social media) can yield to being a wise electorate.

The table exists when we do our best to love our neighbors as ourselves (treat others as we want to be treated) and support what is best for the common good.

We see its power to make our nation better, whether in the halls of government, at a peaceful protest, at a shelter for battered women, at a neighborhood barbeque, at a Veteran's Day parade, or at See You At The Pole (where students gather to pray for their school).

The publisher of this book has given it a place at the table, to be a part of the discussion about American government, but you don't need a book to join in the conversation. Just bring yourself and your American Dream.

As long as We the People are willing to come to the table and faithfully engage in the process, our combined efforts in behalf of the Preamble of the Constitution shall not be found wanting.

# Postscript

*The Founders themselves were vigorous critics of the wisdom they had inherited and the principles in which they believed. They were articulate, opinionated individuals who loved to examine ideas - to analyze, argue, and debate them. They expected no less of future generations. They would expect no less of us. ***

*Reprinted with permission. We the People: The Citizen and the Constitution, Level 3. Copyright Center for Civic Education. Calabasas, California, www.civiced.org.

www.ingramcontent.com/pod-product-compliance
Lightning Source LLC
Chambersburg PA
CBHW060404050426
42449CB00009B/1899